Light and Dark

Light and Dark

Poems by

Alex Barr

© 2024 Alex Barr. All rights reserved.
This material may not be reproduced in any form, published,
reprinted, recorded, performed, broadcast,
rewritten, or redistributed without
the explicit permission of Alex Barr.
All such actions are strictly prohibited by law.

Cover image by Rosemarie Barr
Author image by Rosemarie Barr

ISBN: 978-1-63980-623-2

Kelsay Books
502 South 1040 East, A-119
American Fork, Utah 84003
Kelsaybooks.com

To Rosemarie

with love

Acknowledgments

Poems in this collection previously appeared in the following journals:

14 Magazine: "Too Deep"
Acumen: "In Praise of Sheds"
BlueHouse Journal: "Voices"
Culture Cult Magazine: "Life Lines," "How Peculiar to meet Mr Barr"
The Dark Horse: "Daffodil Ride"
The Frogmore Papers: "Speed Date" (shortlisted for the Frogmore Prize)
Hole in the Head Review: "Not You," "Nutcracker"
Last Stanza Poetry Journal: "Ipsissimus"
Light Magazine: "Classical Clerihews"
The MacGuffin: "Keats Has a Line"
Orbis: "Too Far"
The Plaza Prize Anthology: "More Than I Bargained For" (shortlisted for the Plaza Prize)
Poetry Review: "Notes for the Bean of Beans"
Scintilla: "Ash," "Letters to My Daughter," "Light and Dark," "German Girl in Old Castile," "Iain"
Silver Birch Press: "There Has to be a Morning"
Southernmost Point Guest House Anthology: "Southernmost Point Guest House," "My Blue Express"
Third Wednesday Journal: "Kudum!"

Contents

Ipsissimus	13
Nutcracker	15
Voices	18
More Than I Bargained For	20
Light and Dark	23
Killers	24
6.15 Leaving Town	25
Basement	26
A Welsh Valediction	28
Too Far	29
Dinner at the 'Olive Branch'	31
Rest	32
Life Lines	34
How Peculiar to Meet Mr Barr	35
This Will Pass	36
'She lay in the long grass'	38
Letters to My Daughter	41
All Souls Day	45
Too Deep	47
Colombella	48
Not You	49
I Ask About Your Night	50
Markers	51
Requiem for a Pot	53
Song for M	54
Epithalamion	55
Daffodil Ride	56
My Blue Express	57
Keats Has a Line	59
Iain	60
In Praise of Sheds	62
Reborn	63
Domes	64

Any Thirty   65
Classical Clerihews   67
Speed Date   68
Signs of Other Lives   69
The Having-a-Lovely-Time Grand Prix   71
German Girl in Old Castile   72
'There has to be a morning'   73
Southernmost Point Guest House   74
Kudum!   75
Ash   76
Embraces   78
Notes for "The Bean of Beans"   79

Ipsissimus

Fiddling with twiddles on some fancy temple
moaning orgasmically, "This is amazing,"
while bemused natives gather, uncertain
whether to look at the camera, or you,
doesn't impress, *Adrasteia.* Your books,
TV series, accolades, weighed in the balance
are wanting because you don't mention the most
remarkable, gemlike, iconic construction:
the big cooling tower in the center of Stockport
(sadly demolished back in the seventies)
Dave and I christened *The Mayor's Pepper Pot.*

Well done, *Dysponteus,* you rowed single-handed
across the Atlantic—a tour de force. BUT
I've one simple question, fairly rhetorical:
have you, my friend, having launched off the slipway
at Lower Town quayside into the calm
but quite swelly briny shielded by breakwaters,
told by the cox, "Come forward to row",
been bumped in the back by Suzanne in the bow?

Poor *Meliboëa,* despite your success,
prizes, prizes, collections, collections,
accolades, motorcades, five-star reviews,
you're laboring under the terrible burden
of not having written that witty and elegant
haiku that showed how the author's camellia
didn't collapse even though he was stressed.

Don't get me started on you, *Dexamenus,*
Oscars for acting *and* scriptwriting, yes,
rogering movie stars, shooting the rapids,
flying a biplane, breeding chihuahuas,
owning a castle, owning an island,
owning Picassos and Brancusi bronzes—
all that I'm asking is: have you a cat
called Louie? *The Life of the Fly* by H. Fabre?
Had the good fortune to sleep with my wife?

Let's praise the achievements of all the above
who mastered the blockage, impediment, obstacle,
grave disadvantage of NOT BEING ME.

Nutcracker

How could T.J.Maxx
sell you for the price
of two cans of lager?

Someone in Eastern Europe
stuck on all your sequins
painted your mustache

carved your golden crown
the domed silver top
of your timekeeping mace

made your moving jaw
to bite down hard on
the stuff I'm sending you:

Crunch it all, crunch it
to free me from blame.
Swallow, swallow
into your wooden wame:

the abandoned polytunnel;
the fruit now someone else's;
the scent of summer meadows;

the show not seen on Broadway;
the show the critics killed;
the show that fouled a friendship;

the writings in the style
of Reverend Casaubon
and William McGonagall;

the kiss I should have given
Fräulein Müller; the kiss
I didn't give Jennifer Ann;

my anger with Angharad;
the cruel scorn I used
to break up with Jane;

the STD I got
from Monserrat; my letter
to Leonie when drunk;

the *porrones* I didn't get
for Don from Mexico;
my mockery of John E;

my useless temperament
for flying; my cowardice
when young Seán was killed;

the house I built
and hardly ever lived in;
the road I should have taken;

the unformed soul
of the child I should have had;
the walks abandoned;

the phone call I forgot
because of my impatience
the day Maisie died;

my torpor over floods,
and hurricanes, and fires;
take all these

as your mace with its beat
keeps time, time, time
in an unrelenting rhyme

and crunch them, crunch,
to free me from shame
swallow them, swallow
into your wooden wame.

Voices

Jim

"The boys next door you played with
in the shed full of rotten apples
or the treehouse in the oak
you reached on rungs of cut-nails
so high above my sickbed—
why did you make them snicker
every time you named me,
near death, as 'Fat Baboon'?"

Tom

"I sat in the ward bemused
(one day you will know the feeling)
no longer whistling *Danny Boy*
too out of tune to please you.
Why did I think you would come?
Your thoughts were with the young
you would feed on golden apples.
You came when my soul had flown."

Marjorie

"Why, the last night of my life,
did you heave up this word, that word
like coals that failed to warm me?
I said, 'I am useless.' You,
'Not at all. I must go.'
'Not yet . . .' 'Look back and think
of your many pleasant years.' And you
with that last effort left me."

L—

"Why when far too late
did you hurry to try to quench
my *Nasty and Horrid* thoughts,
when you took no care to save me
from the sly King of Lies
before it was too late?
Were you worthy of the strange
life I stole from you?"

Milutin, Seán

"How could you misconstrue
my last call to you?"
"I lay dead on the track.
You would not leave the train."
I am coming, my six dears.
In the shadow land I will
right your wrongs. I will
explain, explain, explain.

More Than I Bargained For

"Don't over-pay them," says a fellow tourist,
"otherwise you raise their expectations."
She is American, we are Brits, but we
are the same tribe, the Bargain Vigilantes,
and wield the mighty dollar.

We're in the shoeshine capital of the world,
the capital of soroche (mountain sickness).
We stroll past pavement vendors of minute
potatoes—the odd handful—cigarettes
in ones and twos, and—to ward off spells—
llama fetuses. We pass shop windows
of undertakers piled with white
child-size coffins.

Now we are further north
in the heartland of the Inca
land of hyperinflation
where a bottle of water costs a million inti.
The tour bus stops at a tree-lined plaza
with stalls, and views of alien-looking distance.
We look to haggle.
Here is a gourd with intricate decoration.
"¿*Cuánto?*" He names a price. "¡*Demasiado!*"
We walk away but he runs after
holding the gourd out at the lower price.
The Bargain Vigilantes ride again.

Thirty-two years later
for the first time I study
the ripple of drawings incised in the surface.
So many! Angular figures in procession:
notables with feather crowns,
long robes, elaborate shawls,
and under them, hatted and trousered, smaller figures
I realize are a marching band
with saxophones (or what look like saxophones).
One has a wide fiddle, one a harp.

There is much foliage
around them, and above—
birds. Further round, the agricultural section.
Peons lead llamas through a stylized forest;
others bend to wield mattocks. Two pairs of oxen
are plowing—the new furrows clearly shown.
Further, more peasant farmers bend
to harvest what looks like cane.
Then, where the forest is leafy and dense,
we come full circle and see
the tail end of the band.

My likeness, my fellow artist,
I imagine you bent over the work for hours,
your dark features composed in concentration,
using some kind of burin to engrave
around the neck of the gourd rosettes and points
in geometric patterns, and populate
the miniature crust with creatures.

For years the gourd was a familiar object,
dusty among the ornaments. Forgive
my grudging inattention to your pageant.
When I think of the Bargain Vigilantes
I remember Coppard's story of the Higgler
who lost the love of his life, obsessed with barter,
and bowing down like one of those hatted peons
I dig these words into my crust of guilt.

Light and Dark

Egrets: dazzling white
and buff. Broad heron wings.
Unhurried flapping flight.
Long legs. Long beak for things
like fish. They feed among
heifers or near a bull.
Stress the first syllable
if their name is said or sung.

Regrets: so dark they suck
hues from the sky like ghouls.
Their flight when they attack
is silent as an owl's.
Talons for gripping fast.
Hawk-beaks capable
of shredding flesh. The syllable
for stressing is the last

Killers

Bloodthirsty brutes, you murdered my meadow-pipit.
She came as I weeded, arm's length away, trusting,
rustling the dried-up leaves, busy among the stalks
of nettle and campion, the wires of the periwinkle,
a living ball of energy, thrush-breasted.

Her bright black eye regarded me fearlessly.
I felt at one with the world. And later found her,
sad little handful, unredeemable ball of death,
beak part open as if amazed by this betrayal.
I hope her end was quick. I hope mine will be.

Come, little assassins, and snuggle up beside me.
Your fur is warm and the night is far from tender.
My colonial ancestors annihilated humans
they saw as a different species. So like you
I belong to a breed of bewhiskered killers.

6.15 Leaving Town

They've such bold noses to them
the three striding there along the platform.

The man's profound, Assyrian-bearded, powerful.
The woman's a Portuguese princess. Her hair falls

in two dense curtains. The daughter I divine as
a girl of character before they vanish.

My rail-fellows, flopjawed, with flabby eyes
languish. I loll among them, compromised.

Basement

Nobody suffered in it,
not even the cleaner, Lily,
the day my sister and I locked her in
for mispronouncing our names.
She fluttered against the door
so feebly it surprised us, but of course
there was nothing down there to fear.

Plain wooden shelves held empty jam jars.
Mother, busy with Gran, no longer filled them.
I missed the sweat in her hairline as she stirred,
the streaks of brilliant crimson down the copper.
But those planks never creaked under debris
from wasted projects, letters and photographs
from failed loves, the possessions of the dead.

One lightless room was always under
an inch of water. I used to trick my friends
to make them tread in it.
In the war it was used as an air-raid shelter
but unlike 'Beaconsfield' round the corner
our house was never hit by Hitler's bombers.
Nobody suffered. No child was crushed.

On the big stone table
friends and I settled
a wooden 'pin' of beer for a party
hoping our mastery
of *shive, spile,* and *spigot*
and mild intoxication would impress
the girls. We had yet to be mortified
by jealous anger, drunken lust,
transmittable disease.

The air was cool, and smelt
of stone, damp earth, and mildew.
You could leave the door from the kitchen wide:
there was nothing down there to fear,
nothing to make you suffer.
Time had forgotten the rust on the shelf supports,
the flakes of distemper littering the floor.
Only the dials
of the dusty meters ticked and whirred.

A Welsh Valediction

Farewell the six green acres of Parc y Glyn
down whose steep end we tobogganed riding bin-bags
and no-one but John Young dared drive a tractor.
Farewell the only level ground of our holding, where
stood the marquee for our anniversary.

Farewell the six-and-a-half grassy acres
of Parc Gwaunglawdd Uchaf where for weeks
we bottle-fed Ellie the orphan lamb
till the fox took her. Farewell the stream
chuckling beside the one majestic beech tree.

Farewell the buzzards piping to their young
the swerving swallows who announced the spring
and lined the power lines for departure.
Farewell the scent of hay meadows adorned
with bird's foot trefoil, yellow rattle, self-heal.

Farewell the bales of hay, their old-gold color.
Farewell the jagged horizon in the sunset.
Farewell eating bread in the sweat of faces.
Farewell knowing who we were: smallholders.
Farewell to youth, and with many thanks, to life.

Too Far

To live like Ian and Linda
under a thundering outcrop
would be something . . .

Its vertical pearl grey strata
born in red roaring depths
straining for heaven

a bundle of silent force
like a cat set to spring.
Watching. Waiting.

Fissures in its jagged outline
trap the sky the way rugged inlets
trap the restless sea.

Like a tooth from a gum
it thrusts clear of gorse,
grass, dwarf hazel, thorn.

Ian and Linda feed on
its grandeur. Things go well
for them, their land, their kinder.

I too have an outcrop—mine
(sharing a name with theirs)
more than three miles away.

I climbed the hill to see it.
What seemed a mere summit mound
was a giant stack of strata

the gold grey and dun of the sky
gripped by its sawteeth.
I blundered toward its base

laid hands on, felt its wonder,
tried to spy in the distance
this house. But could not.

Too far. Too far! Ah
to live like Ian and Linda,
that would be something.

Dinner at the 'Olive Branch'

Dining alone is tough,
tougher than you expected.
You want to leave in a huff.

You order. You sound too gruff.
You feel you're being inspected.
Dining alone is tough,

The others sound happy enough—
too happy. You feel rejected.
You want to leave in a huff.

You study your nails, your cuff,
try not to be affected.
Dining alone is tough.

The table is bare of stuff
like candles. You're unprotected.
You want to leave in a huff,

or suddenly be snuffed
out, then resurrected.
Dining alone is tough.

Your composure is a bluff
that can't go undetected.
You want to leave in a huff.
Dining alone is tough.

Rest

I flourished the day my bench was put together:
inch plywood, baulks of nine by three, firm legs.
(*My* legs hardly raise me from crouching.)

Now I have cut the ends off.
They overhung the legs thirteen inches.
(My stooped head overhangs my body.)

There's emptiness now around it.
Once eight feet long, now five feet ten.
(I was once five eleven. Now five eight.)

The cuts released the smell of parana pine
which took me back to the school woodwork shop.
Memory man, reductio ad absurdum.

A joiner, Ron, who worked on a house I built
made the leg frames. I fell out with him
over a wrong dimension in the kitchen.

I moved a grinder in from the overhang.
She grinds unwanted bits off her ceramics.
(Grinders cease when few, or their owner ceases.)

On the bench lies a seventeen-inch plane
stamped with the names of Granddad and his father.
Each year I shave ambition more and more.

Granddad made a wheelbarrow for my father.
Green-painted wood, beautifully done, with style.
It entertained my son. Where is it now?

What have I made? Mirrors. Equipages:
horses and carts for seven great-grandchildren,
one of whom will inherit Granddad's plane.

My tools are packed: my miter saw, my router,
all my neglected badly-sharpened chisels.
I am empty of projects. Bursting with emptiness.

A man with no project is a drifting cloud.
A man with no project is a rock cast down in the sea.
A man with no project is himself a project.

A man with no project is a turkey's father—
less than that, father of a turkey's ghost,
but he can rest at last, he can rest!

Life Lines

Too many fingers in too many pies,
too many hats I could wear,
too many apples in too many eyes,
too many balls in the air.

Too many irons in too many fires,
not enough pence to the pound,
too many daydreams, too many desires,
not enough feet on the ground.

Too little talent for physics and math,
not enough reading of Rumi,
too many woods with too many a path,
not enough wind blowing through me.

Not enough years left at seventy-three,
far too much business unfinished . . .
Ah, but then *somebody* has to be me,
and has to go on, undiminished.

How Peculiar to Meet Mr Barr

How peculiar to meet Mr Barr
who thinks of himself as still young
even though he's a great-grandpapa
and his swan-song's about to be sung.

How tedious to hear him complain
that he wasted his time as a lad,
or wish that he looked like a star
when he looks more and more like his dad.

How especially annoying to hear him
claim some expertise in poetics:
a subject he's no more au fait with
than sheep-shearing or cybernetics.

Don't listen if he should relate
his struggles with vectors and alge-
bra, but leave him alone to his fate
with his silences and his nostalgia.

This Will Pass

I can't go on and on like this
it can't continue as it is
the status quo's ephemeral
my state is not perpetual

each moment offers something new
I could be looking forward to
the present isn't carved in wood
oh nothing is the same for good

life goes in phases like the moon
a waning is expected soon
conditions now—they just can't last
the variables are varying fast
it won't be long till this has passed

> *another day, another day*
> *the wind will blow another way*

I can't go on and on like this
the situation isn't fixed
chance will amend the way it is
a new condition must be next

the random always plays a role
the juncture judders to a turn
the reader's hand unwinds the scroll
the Heraclitian fire will burn

the freezing fog will start to lift
occurrences will cause a shift
the finger writes and moves along

no circumstance is here for long
a change of key relieves the song

> *another day, another day*
> *your presence will have less to say*

life isn't baked inside a crust
no circumstance is cast in bronze
I'm not dug in like standing stones
the screws that screw me down will rust

things-as-they-are will never stay
the context has to come ungummed
events are not completely jammed
you will belong to yesterday

there's not a road that doesn't bend
the scribbling finger scribbles more
no situation can endure
somehow your ending has to end

a different set-up's on the way
and what arose will pass away
the Zeit must have another Geist
with steam or spray instead of ice
it all can alter in a trice

> *another day, another day*
> *the wind will blow your flowers away.*

'She lay in the long grass'

She lay in the long grass and saw nothing
but blue in the zenith, polished immortal blue,
the original, the unstained, the ancient blue,
the friendly firmament
under which she had always lived,
under which she now lay, breathing
and gazing up at the celestial sphere, while
timothy, sweet vernal grass, and meadow foxtail waved
their seed heads at the limits of her vision.
Their grace, their elusive scent, made her smile,
keen to resume her life's work after rest.
And seeing in the zenith: nothing.

In the second slice of time there was nothing
riding the zenith, unless (imagination?)
a mote, an impurity, a glitch, a grain
set in the blue like a dark flaw in a sapphire,
an otherwise perfect sapphire.
No seeds of foxtail or sweet vernal grass
had floated onto her pupils. The wind had stilled,
resting like her before resuming, and yes
when she blinked and rubbed her eyes and looked again
the dark thing was real, still in place
at the limit of her vision like a stain
on the blue zenith where there had been nothing.

In the third slice of time there was nothing
but simple joy. High in the zenith hovered
something alive with wings that trembled
(the speck had grown), and the watcher trembled—

not through fear, but as one who sees a lover
after long absence waving blindly, getting
close, and remembers how that person filled
her heart, and remembers after long forgetting
the subtle taste of his kiss, as delicate as the taste
of a fresh pulled stalk of summer grass—
trembled to see the skylark she thought the thing resembled
in the blue zenith where there had been nothing.

In the fourth slice of time there was nothing
when she closed her eyes but the sound of wings
and the stirring of the grasses beside his face.
When she opened them it was still there above her,
the dark, winged being, not of the human race.
Its presence didn't surprise her altogether—
perhaps she had already imagined that silhouette
whose features were lost in shadow against the blue.
Its height above her was hard to estimate;
she couldn't tell the size of its deeply indented wings,
and as for divining whether
it was a cold automaton, or warm and living,
nothing betrayed its nature, nothing.

In the fifth slice of time there was nothing
more to be done. Each time she turned her head
to look past the flattened grass at the horizon
she saw, below a dark mass, a line of crimson
such as she had seen before when the sun, sinking
peeped below a compacted mass of cloud.

The unmoving air was thick with an unknown scent
that was not the scent of a lover, or of the curled
smoke from a leaf bonfire, or of a creature dead.
When she looked up there was nothing
to see in the velvet blackness: no more blue,
and even the crimson band was shrinking
under the wings that covered the world
until at last there was nothing.

Letters to My Daughter

1

Hawking says time, elastic
and hooked like a cycle bungee,
can suddenly snap back:

I tap the brass fox knocker.
Hello from the Asian boys
going in and out next door.

Your variegated laurel.
Your rippled glass.
Your shape blurred in the hall.

Tall I remember. Warm
embrace, that too. Face
an identikit from my album.

2

"Two trailing arms, excessive
wear." An arcane sketch
of drums and linkages.

How long has this gone on?
you wrote under the list
of faults to your car. Someone

perhaps was cheating you?
You put the question twice.
Someone was cheating you?

You are not bound to answer.
Tell me instead how long
you mean to keep this absence.

3

How long can this go on?
Two thousand seven hundred
and eighty-four days gone

since the last time we met.
How beautiful you were.
Forgive how little I said.

But how could you listen then,
smug, nose in the air,
party feet turned in?

Spring. The borders packed
with scents. My plan to forget
your coldness blocked.

4

Are you everywhere?
Did I see you today
at twenty-five to four

in Fishguard Square engrossed
in the eyes of the baby
you carried against your chest?

I saw the brick paving
in many colours. Blood
ash bone liver.

In the mirror I am not old.
I seem to take after you
as if I were *your* child.

5

Shall we be meeting soon
when the white owl flies
out of the creaking barn?

Or at the bluestone gate
below Carningli where
the forest path comes out?

Will you amaze with a rustle
of dead hag's-taper stalks
the garden at Picton Castle

and when the new year chimes
argue with me there
beside the clumps of thyme?

6

A window colored to show
a sailing ship at sunset.
Framed rules. No music, no.

Neck weals carefully hidden
by silk. Around one wrist
a colorful braid ribbon.

Smug, nose in the air.
Why do we never meet?
Or are you everywhere?

The moon is above the barn.
Smell: I'm planing wood.
Listen: the wind is calm.

All Souls Day

I strain with unsteady
imaginary tread
up the stone steps
the thirty-seven steps
up from the cathedral
hiding in its hollow
up from the cathedral
you knew so well.
Slow, slow, breathless
(listen!) I climb those steps
those thirty-seven steps
between banks of grass
set with fallen headstones
towards the gateway
in the ancient wall.
The rooks are strangely silent
the wind at rest.
In the gateway
framed by darkness—you.
I see you beckon
or maybe simply wait
long braid over your shoulder, with
that gentle quizzing look
and ghost of a smile.
Drawn as if by music
lighted windows
the scent of incense
I strain with unsteady
imaginary tread
up the stone steps
the thirty-seven steps
up from the cathedral

towards where you stand
framed by dark
towards the moment
when you will take my arm and lead me through.

Too Deep

I find in the car we gave you
the glasses with cherry rims
you wore when you passed your test
and I think of your eyes whose green
gaze I could never hold.

Daffodils flash their yellow
heralding your birthday.
What brings the bulbs to life?
The sun's touch on the soil?
The percolating showers?

Nothing restores your eyes,
too deep for the rain of tears,
too deep for the heat of anger
that the gift of life we gave you
one Easter was unwanted.

Colombella

He lost her songs and laughter
and wandered empty streets.
Oh, he was wise thereafter
but he bore her like a brand

and never knew what she was after
when she tried to make him understand
and the toy boats she placed in his hand
he thought were enemy fleets.

Not You

I'm sitting in *Drive & Shine*
waiting.
They're valeting our car.
While I wait I think
of the clothes you left on the bathroom floor. Your shell,
your carapace. Not you, but redolent:
the jumper from the Swedish list
with its pattern of stylized daisies, pink
on a buff and sable background,
the corduroy plum-shade trousers with streaks
of raku clay where you wiped your hands,
cream knickers, yellow T-shirt,
the black socks you say I borrow by mistake.

You left this heap so you could come to bed
without disturbing me when I was sleeping.
Yes, one of us has always gone
ahead, and here in *Drive & Shine* I wonder
which of us will find a pile of clothing
one day soon with no body left to fill them.
Who will have gone ahead into the world of light?
Or dark. Or dark.

And here in the bardo waiting-room I murmur,
"My love, O my love, we must meet again,
shining, valeted." Beyond the doorway
an enigmatic frame of girders
partly painted orange, with a rack
of unguents and volatiles for cars
and grubby hoses casually draped
has beauty.

I Ask About Your Night

We drink coffee in our dressing-gowns.
You tell me about the novel you're reading.
It's set in Maine. A novel you're enjoying
in which forty-two Fahrenheit is mentioned.
You ask, "What's that in Celsius?"
Taking me back to those
cold mornings in the school science block,
the dark brown teacher's bench with its taps and Bunsen burner.
I venture, "Six," but you check: "Five point five."

Most of the characters, you say, are poor. I remind you
of the free movie show in Provincetown,
the downtrodden audience. "I felt embarrassed,"
you say, "as if we had no right to be there."
In the novel a disturbed young man
throws a pig's head into a mosque, and the theme
focuses much on tension with Somalis.

You go on reading
in your pink cotton terry dressing-gown. I sit close
watching that look of cosmic concentration—
eyebrows slightly raised as if what you read
is unexpected, which is of course the sign
of good writing. I sit close. I ask about your night.
"I slept quite well, though at some point I woke
my arm across you. Did you notice?" "No,
I wish I had." One day
one of us will read this again and cry.

Markers

We are on the Red Route
through the forest, and this is good, because
we dare not risk being lost. If we were still
midway the journey of our lives we might not care
but now we are near the end. Oh not too near—
we can still walk, and we are still together.

So this is the true path
paved with a palimpsest of oak leaves
burnt sienna, burnt umber, bronze.
It's February. The forest is full of sky.
In June under foliage newly minted
it will be dark. But we will come again
lovers of oak, of druids, of gold leaves
on the caps of high-ranking officers, of legends,
of ancient tree-trunks swaddled in moss.

There are many diverging paths. We wonder
which we should have taken. But the Blue Route
is far too long, both Green and Brown too hilly,
Yellow too short. Yes, yes, Red is best,
we insist, Red is best. And now we are near
the end of our walk, the end of our exploring
which could hardly be called exploring—
merely following arrows on red discs
on hardwood posts around the looping path.

To arrive where we started—that is our aim now. But
where are the Red markers? Are we lost,
seeing this part of the forest
for the first time?
Will we exhaust ourselves
finding a long route back?

But wait, here is a notice: *Coppicing*
of oaks has recommenced,
the timber is used for crafts, or left to rot
for use by woodland creatures.
The sign we passed at the outset
or another? One saying: *Coppicing*
of oaks has recommenced. The black dor beetle
is often seen crossing the paths in summer.

Requiem for a Pot

Wind, envious Wind, *you* did it.
Shunted it off the garden table at seventy miles an hour
so it shattered in fifteen fragments.
Brother Wind, I know the embitterment
that made you break that beautiful plant-pot holder:
"All *I* create is damage and destruction." But
remember you fill sails, drive great turbines,
and sigh beautifully in treetops.

Wind, I watched her make it,
experimenting beyond her usual style.
Oh, she makes a lot of plant-pot holders
but that one was unique:
flared at the rim, incurving at the base,
made in a mold where she pressed curls of clay
coated with colored slips—vermilion, white,
turquoise, olive green, sienna yellow—
and when it dried pulled it out, and inside the rim
incised swirls of white, with her characteristic look
of elegant concentration.

Envious of this poem, Brother Wind
(who scatter my pens but can do nothing with them)?
Trying to snatch it off the garden table
and shred it among the treetops?
Your rancor is misplaced. *My* work is ephemeral.
But the pot you broke—ah, in a thousand years
some archaeologist will excavate the shards
and find the shapes as fresh, the colors as bright as ever.

Song for M

I'm going to hold on and on
while we no longer meet.
I'm going to live with the threat
of eternal separation.

I study your photograph.
Futile. Your features freeze.
But sometimes on the breeze
I almost hear you laugh.

Those big parabolic dishes
at Jodrell Bank, fifty yards
apart, made our whispered words
so clear! And how auspicious

that day seems when I phone
and the conversation drags
like a fire of unseasoned logs
and you'd rather be left alone.

I'm going to hold on through
the scenes of life, as in
the story of Tam Lin.
I believe, I believe in you

as I blunder in dark and mist
in search of the keys I lost
with a torch that seems to have died.
The stars have disappeared

but I know, I know they're up there
enduring patiently
till the marvelous moment they
are ready to reappear.

Epithalamion

for James and Charlie

It is a strange thing to marry.
For beings to bind themselves one-to-one

with skeins of pure white silk, blue ribbons, chains
of fairy gold. The bonds invisible.

Too tightly wound? Too loose? How will you know?
You cannot see. You hope all will be well.

You cannot comprehend or calculate
the flexibility—till one

chasing a mirage threatens to pull the other
off balance. And you measure the breaking strain

only if one falls over a cliff edge, say—the other
taking the precious weight.

*

What do I wish for you?
Your bonds light and lasting as dragline silk

from spider spinnerets seen at dawn
as dew-pearl necklaces on hawthorn branches

which even heavy rain leaves intact.
So flexible it can increase its length

by twenty-seven percent without a break.
As strong as steel. And tougher.

Daffodil Ride

Today is your first birthday in heaven.
On earth you would be ninety. This afternoon I rode
from Middle Mill to Whitchurch—hard, uphill—
then passed the abandoned airfield, empty
of the Eisteddfod, empty of lovely August.
The sky was colorless, and nothing moved until
innumerable starlings like a wave
swirled and shimmered down to sanctify
the sad fields with life.

At the Cathedral, passing the Deanery,
I remembered how I pushed your wheelchair
up the steep blacktop path. The precious weight of you
not to be spilled. Spilled now. And the daffodils were out
on the lawn of Bwthyn-y-Tŵr. And I lit a candle
and another man lit a candle
(but neither asked who the other was lighting for)
and we carried them south passing the shrine
of Dewi Sant into the other transept
(the one you and I once lit candles in)
and the other man placed his on
the middle tier of the black rack. Not wishing
to elevate or downgrade you I placed yours
on the same tier as his.

And there was a book in which one asked for prayers
for those in pain or trouble. *My friend is dying
of cancer,* was one. *He will leave two young boys.
Pray for him.* So I prayed. And realizing you are so filled with love
you have no need of prayer, I left, and rode away.

My Blue Express

I wish I still had the train my father made
with those blunt square hands that saved
string from parcels, punished lying, plied
a rake. That were white and puffy when he died.

After the war, when toys were hard
to find, he carved the engine like the *Mallard:*
a streamlined sloping front, fairings to hide
the cylinders curving gracefully either side

but short like a tank engine. It had no motor.
Maybe he thought that could be added later
from Basset-Lowke's wonder-catalogue. Wheels,
figures with luggage, signal gantries, rails

never arrived. There were two carriages,
cornflower blue like the engine. The edges
of the sides against the roof were imperfect
in spite of careful sanding—which I liked

because it showed exactly how they were made.
I could pull off the roofs and sides to lay
the travellers' domain bare for inspection.
One carriage had space for a guard and parcels.

There were side corridors and compartments
just as in forties films. Facing seats
were covered in thin felt, emerald green.
He and I never talked about the train.

I admired it, rather than played with it, alone,
imagined it clacking across the Nullarbor Plain
or climbing the endless loops towards Darjeeling
(journeys I've yet to take). And did he fling

my blue train away, uncared for, when
at last he was able to buy me a clockwork one?
On my bench lie some of the tools he left me,
sunlit, the handles gleaming softly.

I wish that I could say to him that now I know
how things we make can show with each squeeze of glue,
each stroke of saw and hammer, each coat of varnish,
love we can find no other way to publish.

Keats Has a Line

We roamed for hours. Along scented lanes
unravished by the bypass or the builder
we spoke of love and its attendant pains
and hopes that we forgot as we grew older.

The Cat Girl played her piano unaware
that in the cold and dark we watched and lingered
long, to admire her profile and her hair
and longed to be caressed by those fine fingers.

"Keats has a line in *Lamia,*" Martin said,
"about the summer heaven, blue and clear
between two marble shafts, seen from a bed
made sweet by use." His words fell on my ear
richly. And rich the memory of that year
now I am old and tired and worn, and he is dead.

Iain

The tall, tall, slim French boy stood
in the rain with his back to me, his head
snug in a hood, watching clouds
throw shadows on Pen Caer. I thought
for a moment it was Iain, my friend Iain
(two i's in his name) alive again.

In his attic we pulled out 78s and there
I first heard *When They Begin the Beguine*
that voluptuous tune. One voluptuous night
we played strip poker with the delicious nieces
of Mrs Lichfield. (Very little flesh
got exposed.) We chased them round the garden—
Iain's idea. Next day I said
he'd acted like a fool. "Did *they* say that?"
he countered. "No, they didn't."

In his basement and my washhouse
we messed with flowers of sulfur
potassium permanganate, zinc,
and hydrochloric acid, and he told me
that Norma, whom we met on the cricket field
and whom I ached for, really fancied me.
It was a lie.

Late one afternoon
returning to the Scout camp from a hike
(it seems we lost the rest of our patrol)
he made us do a three-mile detour
along a country lane. I counted telegraph poles
to deal with weariness. When I complained he said,
with all the authority of his extra year,
"Scouts do things the hard way."

In Bogville Private Army
(we were eleven then) he was a lance-jack
but later in the Queen's Own Khaki Squaddies
only a private. Nonetheless he claimed,
"I'm dating the Colonel's daughter."
Was *that* a lie? I see him saying it,
hair butchered by the regimental barber,
tall, horse-faced, outside the Jolly Sailor
with great aplomb. On that same spot
I learned that he had died, at forty-two.

The French boy turned, Garn Fawr beyond his head,
and oh, he wasn't Iain.

In Praise of Sheds

In the glow of a paraffin lamp from 'Spick and Span'
master of my domain long ago
in the old rocking chair
that ground the floorboards in a heavy rhythm

busy with some childish occupation,
humming the ancient hymns I believed in
I watched through the open doorway
the shimmer of sunset poplars.

Such is the memory. Now in this other shed
the door is shut. My gaze is down.
In the light from a dusty window a polished beetle
pursues a pressing mission. A downy moth

flutters beside the wrapper of a tube of mints.
I raise my head and see on the grey planed uprights
ghosts of vanished brackets,
rust-flower lines of screw-heads.

Heat of the day has made the wood aromatic.
Air through knot-holes tickles the dust
and stirs the familiar scent
of creosote to remind me of my father.

The joints in the boards are staves of music
with arpeggios of knots, the rattling door
the call of a kettledrum, the whispering breeze
the echo of a far-off song.

Three narrow shelves hold mustard tins of nails,
abandoned bike lamps, labels of long dead plants.
On simple hooks are weeding tools and brushes.
I hang my griefs among them.

Reborn

after Baudelaire

At Vision Source, amid the bustle and din
I gaze into the eyes of a young woman
who checks the functioning of my new glasses—
"Look in my left. And now look in my right,"

while she writes notes with an exquisite hand.
Ancient voluptuary, I'm lost in those
gray irises, pale harbingers of storm,
sensing a haunting sweetness, fatal pleasure,

rattled as if by lightning. Your look
made me, oh, feel reborn, but I must go
back to the empty atmosphere of age.

If we meet again it will only be as patient
and practitioner . . . or maybe never,
you whom I would have loved, you who knew it.

Domes

The deafening street roars all around us
(Merci pour cette ligne, M. Baudelaire).
Colleague Ted and I rush to dodge
Vespas and Fiats orbiting the Duomo

whose 45-meter width across the drum
was built to rival the Pantheon's 43.
But how construct the dome? No-one ever
built an octagonal one so enormous.

    Oh would it ever
    oh would it ever
    oh would it ever
    ever be possible?

Enter Filippo Brunelleschi who solved
the problem with huge hollow ribs of stone
inside one of which we climb
the many steps and emerge onto the Lantern.

Colleague Ted and I catch our breath
at distant hills and red roofs way below us.
Ted points excitedly. On a third-floor terrace
two young florentines lie soaking sun

domes of their breasts bare to the Tuscan sky.
Lothario Ted says, "Wow, good enough to eat
and meet, but on the ground it all looks different.
In that maze, how would I find that building?"

    Oh would it ever
    oh would it ever
    oh would it ever
    ever be possible?

Any Thirty

to Brahim el-Bakraoui, suicide bomber,
Zaventem Airport, Brussels, March 2016

Peace be upon you, friend
and on your brother
though that will take . . . aeons.

We in the West, you say, stole the kernel
from your life and left a husk—
the husk you trashed on Tuesday.

So it was logical
to claim the lives of thirty
you hold complicit?

And as we are *all* complicit—
infants, old, rich, poor, fit, disabled—
any thirty would answer.

The night before your doom, I went
to a poetry evening
alone. And sat alone.

And no-one approached
or invited me to read.
It seemed they all knew each other.

Another time I dined
alone in a restaurant
sad among jovial crowds.

And did I hate?
Oh hardly. A spark perhaps.
The least of embers, which

I try to imagine blown
by the bellows of some injustice
to a furnace. But I fail.

And yet that ember
is in me, was in the thirty.
Peace be upon them, friend.

Brahim, I feel for your father,
I who have lost a child
to self-inflicted death.

Wherever you are, alone
surrounded by your dead
peace may be a long time coming.

Classical Clerihews

Julius Caesar
won the battle of Alesia.
He thought every Roman would be his friend,
which shows although successful you can come to a messy end.

Polyphemus
thought he wouldn't seem as
absurd and comical
with a contact lens instead of a monocle.

Andromeda
didn't need a thermometer
to know she was blue with cold in the nuddy,
then Perseus came. Embarrassed, she turned hot and ruddy.

Achilles
gave the Trojans the willies:
he strode around the battlefield roaring loud and hulking
when he wasn't sulking.

Nausicaa
lived on Corfu, or maybe Sicily or even Corsica.
She didn't sign her work, through modesty,
but may be the real author of *The Odyssey.*

Helen (Mrs Menelaus)
never meant to cause chaos
and wished instead of launching a thousand ships
she'd stayed home to write *Helen's Handy Household Tips.*

Circe
was told "Men are swine" by Nursie.
Growing up she thought, "Sod metaphor—
literal is what men are better for."

Speed Date

"I am not," Shena said, "Santa Cruz del Islote
with too little open space. A person
should have undeveloped areas, don't you think?
Nor am I"—she shuddered—"Aogashima,
defended by escarpments, with a crater.
I would always avoid a crater, in which you sit
staring at the rim, seeing nothing more,
everything gone. Nor am I Elliðaey
with its lonely house in an expanse of grass.
No trees for birds, and the ones that pass overhead
in skeins would be the thoughts
that leave you empty. Nor am I Torcello—
too accessible. Don't you think a person
should not be too accessible?
Oh but you like the Basilica. Let me tell you
my spirituality can't be shown on walls.
Am I Nihomachi? No. Nice woods,
but home to far too few. Not Papa Westray.
No airstrip for me—if you want to reach me
be slow. Ah, time and metaphor allocation
running out. Let's say I'm Jumo then.
If you were Iniö you would be nice and close.
I'm joking. Over to you.
You've got your two minutes before the bell."

Signs of Other Lives

How they entertain us. We have seen
a stuffed chihuahua, Mexican sarapes,
seven-pound dumbbells, hoards of plastic trophies,
a cat asleep in an empty hanging basket,
photographs of the young in mortarboards,
a kilim with a stain that could be blood,
a glass case full of barbers' implements,
a horse's skull on a shelf in a musty vault,
cushions we were told came from Petra,
kitsch ceramic owls with mournful eyes,
and sad boxes of incontinence pads
that weren't hidden before we came a-viewing.

But this house, the one we're seeing now
has nothing to intrigue us.
The realtor taking us round is cagy.
One of the vendors is outside in tears,
the other invisible. So, why are they selling
with such an air of angst and acrimony?

Ah, maybe there was a secret viewing
while one was away nursing a dying parent.
This viewer would not be greeted
by a smooth-talking realtor but instead
with coffee, cake, warm wet kisses,
the luxury of burgundy bedroom curtains
(matching the velvet dress of a china doll),
lamps with crystal shades,
oval looking-glass in a frame of hammered copper,
book on ferns lying open,
de-luxe Berber rug, a sanctuary
for the bare feet of two,
and under a William Morris duvet cover, ah—
a pink percale sheet of the finest weave.

If there *was* such a secret, it's out.
How will the vendors live without their Eden?
Will they picture our pleasure in the view
of the chapel across the road, the jagged skyline
of larches? Will they cry as they imagine
us tearing down partitions down, re-tiling,
covering empty walls with aquatints and weavings?
Will they remember how the garden,
overgrown, awaited shears, feeding, love?

The Having-a-Lovely-Time Grand Prix

Here are the team results.
No points for the Atterburys
who failed to see the checkered flag
in yet another race.
Margaret lost her job at the garden center.
Les's hip replacement
was cancelled yet again.
Still no sign where any points might come from.
Margaret sighed, "The others
were way ahead from the start,"
and Les, "We did our best."

Just three points for the Eggbys.
Fine practice laps under the duvet
promised an exciting start
and the wedding at Hampton Court
should have placed them among the leaders
but Mac became too pally with a bridesmaid
and Sue with designer cocktails.
He went into the pits. She lost control.
A frantic recovery
brought them in fifth and sixth.

Now Team Jones. Rita,
with her lovely water garden
featured on *Gardener's World*
and an article on manure in *The Sunday Times,*
finished second. Starting from pole position
Roger maintained an effortless lead,
inheriting a Tuscan villa
and getting a fat tax rebate
to finish ahead of the pack.
Shake the champers, happy happy Joneses,
and spraaaay the froth!

German Girl in Old Castile

If I were young, desirable, and full
of life beside the Cathedral of Zamora
as this girl is, and if my cell phone
sang like hers with a call from one I love,
like her I would spin for joy.

As an actor is told to inhabit the whole stage
she fills this enormous dance floor
of paving, lit by the red gels of sunset,
with epicycles, a mauve-and-magenta planet
in the formlessness of space.

Speaking, listening, she denies existence
to the gateau-ish domes and buttresses behind her,
to me, and even to her *compañeras* . . .
and far below, beyond the parapet,
to the Duero in its endless plain.

'There has to be a morning'

There has to be a morning
(one at least among nearly thirty thousand)
where niggles fall
into the Great Melting Pot of Niggles
and there is a sense of lightness
not the fragile lightness of balloons,
more the floating of clouds that just don't mind
where they are heading.

And you notice that Victorian thing you found
("A scent bottle," she says—news to me)
with its glass pointed stopper (like
the top of a stupa, yes?) and elegant swelling body
of cut glass, which you formerly
consigned (along with much of what you wrote)
to the Oubliette of the Useless
along with a heavy heap of Victorian values
and specialized kitchenware: mustache cups,
piping-bag holders, grapefruit spoons . . .

And from the old green wooden box of dusters
and shoe cream you dig out the long-forgotten
Goddard's Long-term Silver Polish, while
the garden (which usually feels too small)
seen through the window is peaceful, without wind,
neat and rectangular, birdless (but so be it),
and you shake the bottle and follow the instructions
and rub and rub and chain back to those mornings
when Billiken God of Things As They Ought To Be
took charge and sent the dour distractions off
to the Desert of Enduring Emptiness,
and although the sky is a blank
tapestry of gray, the neck of that useless thing,
Victorian thing, has come alive with light.

Southernmost Point Guest House

The night is giving itself such airs—
heavy scents not quite incense.
Beyond the black cutout leaves and hanging roots
of a giant ficus tree, a lighted window
is sliced by the horizontals of a blind.
A cock in the distance crows
into the deep recesses of the dark.

Leaving Europe I strained against my seat-belt,
saw the gray wing with its *fault access cover,*
wanted home, the ducks driven late to bed,
the stove red in the dark, the heat of your sleeping back.
I thought of the Ten Perfections one by one.
My death sat quiet in the seat beside me
patiently, having swallowed all the ones
I dream I might have been.

Here I'm alive among a million leaves,
a hundred lights. Let them all come,
those ghosts of unriddled selves—
editor, preacher, artist, activist—
with all their thirst and clinging
like bats around this little balcony
crowding this brief scene in a different life
until at last they vanish
into the proud night that will devour them.

Kudum!

Okay, their empire didn't suit everyone
especially near the end when it turned nasty
and their sultans often murdered their younger brothers
and I'm guilty of Orientalism, but
indulge me for a moment because
here in traffic-congested Istanbul
the music these guys are making
is sizzling all my sinews.

If they marched I'd follow
sporting a long embroidered robe like theirs
and a tall crimson cylinder hat draped with fine white cotton
or maybe a giant onion of a turban
to the beat of that pair of drums.

I like the way the drummer looks up to the side
whenever he twirls his sticks
looking at what? Who knows? Doesn't miss a beat
and I'm touched by his patent pride
but his youthful beard is nothing
to the thundering wide mustache of the older man beside him
(a scimitar in his belt) crashing cymbals.
Four others are crashing cymbals,
while the timekeeper thumps the paving with his staff.

But what's really killing me
is the sound of those long black pipes I think
are called *kavals* or *zurnas*.
Do I say their notes are throaty? Mournful? Harsh?
Or simply give up describing them, because
the main thing is they make me want to march
in a glittering pageant waving a long silk banner
blazoned with gold calligraphy like snakes. *Kudum*
is the name of that pair of drums. *Kudum, kudum!*

Ash

a sestina

I'm spreading ash from the fire
on the yard, in a snaking pattern
from a carrier bag onto compacted stones.
It's lucky there's no wind.
The black sky is clear, the stars perfect,
the Plough a signal, Jupiter a torch.

I'm spreading ash in the beam of a torch.
The year is dying. We sit before the fire
consoling ourselves that nothing is ever perfect.
Weeping and laughter weave a pattern.
Shriveled leaves are herded by the wind
into the bed of the stream among the stones.

Rain will bed down the ash between the stones
of the yard. I've thrown away the torch
as useless, and now I'm listening to the wind
in the chimney stirring the embers of the fire.
Nights and days make a syncopated pattern
that in hindsight may seem perfect.

Parts of the dying year *were* almost perfect.
Children gathered veined and mottled stones
to arrange on the garden steps in a pattern
they understood. At night we used a torch
to hunt for slugs and mushrooms. The fire
wasn't needed. We flew kites in a gentle wind.

Remember all that, remember! While the wind
tears at the trees and sings a perfect
anthem of solitude. Stoke up the fire,
carry the ash to spread among the stones,
remember to buy a more reliable torch,
gaze at the heavens's undeciphered pattern.

Our lives are embedded in the endless pattern
of generations borne along by the wind
of Time. If we are bearers of the torch
of hope and wisdom, we are no less perfect
than those who raised the rings of standing stones,
measured the lunar months, and discovered fire.

Ash from our stove will make a perfect
bed for our footsteps there among the stones
we tread to search for logs to stoke the fire.

Embraces

Sea, dear Sea, we thank you for your gifts:
infinity of restless reflections of sunlight,
infinity of white combers (those 'horses'),
infinity of odd creatures known and unknown,
your gentle breathing heard in darkness.

Notes for "The Bean of Beans"

I'm planning a dithyramb
or something like it
entitled "The Bean of Beans"
evoking my search
in a loose flowing style as if the author
was weaned on the Beat Poets
not the Church Hymnary.

Free of constraints of form
the verse will symbolize
the freeing of beans from pods. By nesting
the lines in stanza packets of varying lengths
I'll symbolize the nesting of the beans
in pods of varying sizes,
and in the podlike poem as a whole
each stanza will stand for a bean.

To dramatize the search for perfection,
its problems, its disappointments,
I'll bring to the reader's mind Sir Percival
sweating uphill in clunky armor
in search of the Grail . . . or Faust
in Boito's *Mefistofele* singing,
"Il real fu dolore, e l'ideal fu sogno". . .
or Plato, mosquito-bitten, sweating in Syracuse,
telling young Dionysius the dictator
that geometry is a greater delight
than sex, or quail stuffed with figs.

These allusions will add class
but if they seem too recherché
I'll temper them with a conceit
on the beans themselves (borlotti)
comparing the soft lining of their pods
to the skin of an inner thigh, or the ermine
inside a baronial purse.
(Memo: check—find a baronial purse.)
Pods that are dry and brittle but contain
usable beans will be a metaphor
for my senescence, desiccated, stiff,
but fruitful after a fashion (yes, I like that).

The beans themselves
('bean' will call for elegant variation:
'legume' perhaps, or 'item') I'll characterize
as 'mottled', 'pied', 'striated', 'indistinct',
'with equatorial bands', 'with greyish mold',
or 'dark one side and light the other
like Saturn's moon Iapetus'
hoping to nail the perfect pattern
like Japanese who seek the Koi of Koi
and pay, oh, millions.

I'll show myself in the sun
at a worm-riddled table
popping the pods, fingers stained with juice,
hands aching, remembering afternoons with Mother,
items overflowing her brown bowl.
Busy with other veg
my partner will make appearance
and pause to approve the splitting of a pod.

I'll write, "Some *legumes* huddle in their nests
resenting the light of day, but others
leap out rejoicing to be free." And add,
"Some pods contain eight candidates
for Bean of Beans, arranged
like university rowers. Others
just one—which could be the One."

Depicting the pile of rejects
I'll say that although I failed
to find the Bean of Beans, the sun
was a blessing, Garn Fawr
sat nicely on the horizon
and the day was perfect.

Notes

"Ipsissimus" is in the rhythm known as Alcmanics in homage to Peter Reading.

"Reborn" is a version of the Baudelaire poem *"A Une Passante."*

In "A Welsh Valediction," '*Parc y Glyn*' is Welsh for 'Glyn's Field' and '*Parc Gwaunglawdd Uchaf*' for 'Upper Ditch Meadow Field.'

In "Iain" a 'lance-jack' is slang for lance-corporal, the lowest rank of non-commissioned officer in the British army, Nato code OR-3 equivalent to private first class in the US army.

In "All Souls Day" there are in reality *thirty-nine* steps down to the Cathedral, but that would create the wrong associations, and anyway 'thirty-seven' fits the rhythm better.

About the Author

Alex Barr was born in Manchester, England and educated at Manchester Grammar School. After a haphazard career as bus-conductor, journalist (best job: wire editor of *The Wichita Beacon*), garden laborer, and ice-cream salesman, gained a Diploma in Architecture with distinction from Portsmouth Polytechnic and taught in the Department of Architecture and Landscape at Manchester Polytechnic (now MMU).

On taking early retirement he and his wife Rosemarie, a ceramic artist, moved to a smallholding in West Wales where they struggled with limited success to breed sheep and poultry and grow fruit and vegetables, then moved to Fishguard. The Pembrokeshire landscape has inspired much of his poetry. He is proud to be a father, grandfather, and great-grandfather, and hopes to live long enough for the accolade 'great-great'.

His previous poetry collections are *Letting in the Carnival* from Peterloo (1984) and *Henry's Bridge* from Starborn (2006). His short fiction collection *My Life With Eva* is published by Parthian (2017), his collection of stories for children, *Take a Look at Me-e-e!* by Pont Books (2014). He won third prize in the UK's National Poetry Competition, first prize in the Doolin Writers Short Story Competition in Ireland, and the Susan Hansell Drama Award for his short play *Armor.*